U.K. YEARBOOK

ISBN: 9798713414856

This book gives a fascinating and informative insight into life in the United Kingdom in 1942. It includes everything from the most popular music of the year to the cost of a buying a new house. Additionally, there are chapters covering people in high office, the best-selling films of the year and all the main news and events. Want to know which horse won the Derby or which British personalities were born in 1942? All this and much more awaits you within.

INDEX

FIRST EDITION

1942

January
M	T	W	T	F	S	S
			1	2	3	4
5	6	7	8	9	10	11
12	13	14	15	16	17	18
19	20	21	22	23	24	25
26	27	28	29	30	31	

○:2 ☽:10 ●:16 ☾:24

February
M	T	W	T	F	S	S
						1
2	3	4	5	6	7	8
9	10	11	12	13	14	15
16	17	18	19	20	21	22
23	24	25	26	27	28	

○:1 ☽:8 ●:15 ☾:23

March
M	T	W	T	F	S	S
						1
2	3	4	5	6	7	8
9	10	11	12	13	14	15
16	17	18	19	20	21	22
23	24	25	26	27	28	29
30	31					

○:3 ☽:9 ●:17 ☾:25

April
M	T	W	T	F	S	S
		1	2	3	4	5
6	7	8	9	10	11	12
13	14	15	16	17	18	19
20	21	22	23	24	25	26
27	28	29	30			

○:1 ☽:8 ●:15 ☾:23 ○:30

May
M	T	W	T	F	S	S
				1	2	3
4	5	6	7	8	9	10
11	12	13	14	15	16	17
18	19	20	21	22	23	24
25	26	27	28	29	30	31

☽:7 ●:15 ☾:23 ○:30

June
M	T	W	T	F	S	S
1	2	3	4	5	6	7
8	9	10	11	12	13	14
15	16	17	18	19	20	21
22	23	24	25	26	27	28
29	30					

☽:5 ●:13 ☾:21 ○:28

July
M	T	W	T	F	S	S
		1	2	3	4	5
6	7	8	9	10	11	12
13	14	15	16	17	18	19
20	21	22	23	24	25	26
27	28	29	30	31		

☽:5 ●:13 ☾:21 ○:27

August
M	T	W	T	F	S	S
					1	2
3	4	5	6	7	8	9
10	11	12	13	14	15	16
17	18	19	20	21	22	23
24	25	26	27	28	29	30
31						

☽:4 ●:12 ☾:19 ○:26

September
M	T	W	T	F	S	S
	1	2	3	4	5	6
7	8	9	10	11	12	13
14	15	16	17	18	19	20
21	22	23	24	25	26	27
28	29	30				

☽:2 ●:10 ☾:17 ○:24

October
M	T	W	T	F	S	S
			1	2	3	4
5	6	7	8	9	10	11
12	13	14	15	16	17	18
19	20	21	22	23	24	25
26	27	28	29	30	31	

☽:2 ●:10 ☾:16 ○:24

November
M	T	W	T	F	S	S
						1
2	3	4	5	6	7	8
9	10	11	12	13	14	15
16	17	18	19	20	21	22
23	24	25	26	27	28	29
30						

☽:1 ●:8 ☾:15 ○:22

December
M	T	W	T	F	S	S
	1	2	3	4	5	6
7	8	9	10	11	12	13
14	15	16	17	18	19	20
21	22	23	24	25	26	27
28	29	30	31			

☽:1 ●:8 ☾:14 ○:22 ☽:30

PEOPLE IN HIGH OFFICE

Monarch - King George VI
Reign: 11th December 1936 - 6th February 1952
Predecessor: Edward VIII
Successor: Elizabeth II

Prime Minister

Winston Churchill - Conservative
10th May 1940 - 26th July 1945

Ireland

Canada

United States

Taoiseach Of Ireland
Éamon de Valera
Fianna Fáil
29th December 1937

Prime Minister
Mackenzie King
Liberal Party
23rd October 1935

President
Franklin D. Roosevelt
Democratic Party
4th March 1933

 Australia

Prime Minister
John Curtin (1941-1945)

 Brazil

President
Getúlio Vargas (1930-1945)

 China

Premier
Chiang Kai-shek (1939-1945)

 Cuba

President
Fulgencio Batista (1940-1944)

 Egypt

Prime Minister
Hussein Sirri Pasha (1940-1942)
Mustafa el-Nahhas Pasha (1942-1944)

 France

President
Vacant (1940-1944)

 Germany

Chancellor
Adolf Hitler (1933-1945)

 India

Viceroy of India
Victor Alexander John Hope (1936-1943)

Italy

Prime Minister
Benito Mussolini (1922-1943)

Japan

Prime Minister
Hideki Tōjō (1941-1944)

Mexico

President
Manuel Ávila Camacho (1940-1946)

New Zealand

Prime Minister
Peter Fraser (1940-1949)

Russia

Communist Party Leader
Joseph Stalin (1922-1952)

South Africa

Prime Minister
Jan Smuts (1939-1948)

Spain

Prime Minister
Francisco Franco (1938-1973)

Turkey

Prime Minister
Refik Saydam (1939-1942)
Ahmet Fikri Tüzer (1942)
Şükrü Saracoğlu (1942-1946)

BRITISH NEWS & EVENTS

JAN

The Mildenhall Treasure, a large hoard of 34 masterpieces of Roman silver tableware from the fourth century AD, is discovered by ploughman Gordon Butcher at West Row, near Mildenhall, Suffolk. *NB: The collection is on view today at the British Museum and is a permanent feature of the museum's Romano-British gallery.*

1st — An underground explosion caused by sparks from wagons igniting coal dust at Sneyd Colliery, in the North Staffordshire Coalfield, kills 57 men and boys.

1st — The Book Production War Economy Agreement, an agreement between the government and publishers spelling out standards for paper conservation, comes into force.

8th — Richard Peirse is replaced as Bomber Commands Air Officer Commanding-in-Chief by Air Marshal Arthur Harris.

9th — Miners at the Betteshanger colliery in Kent go on strike when mine owners refuse to pay the previously agreed minimum daily wage; this occurred after the miners were unable to meet management production quotas on a new coalface. *Notes: Under wartime regulations, Order 1305, striking was illegal unless the matter had been referred to the Ministry of Labour and National Service for settlement. Prosecutions were made against the strikers; three union officials were imprisoned and 1,085 men fined. A settlement was reached and the men to returned to work on the 29th January. The imprisoned men received a royal pardon on the 2nd February and the fines were remitted in July 1943.*

10th — The last air raid of the war by the German Luftwaffe on Liverpool destroys several houses on Upper Stanhope Street. By a quirk of fate one of the houses destroyed is number 102, the home of Alois Hitler Jr., half-brother of Adolf Hitler and the birthplace of Hitler's nephew, William Patrick Hitler. *NB: In all during the Liverpool Blitz German bombs killed 2,716 people in Liverpool, 442 people in Birkenhead, 409 people in Bootle, and 332 people in Wallasey.*

25th — The Japanese puppet state Thailand declares war on the United States and the United Kingdom.

26th — The first American troops to enter the European Theatre of Operations land at Dufferin Dock in Belfast, Northern Ireland. *Interesting facts: Between 1942 and the end of the second world war around 300,000 American service personnel passed through Ulster. At its peak, U.S. military personnel made up around a tenth of Northern Ireland's population, and by the end of the war almost 2,000 women from Ulster had become GI brides.*

29th — The BBC Radio 4 programme Desert Island Discs is broadcast on BBC Forces Programme for the first time. Presented by Roy Plomley, Austrian-born British actor and radio comedian Vic Oliver is the first castaway.

FEB

British Army research officer James Stanley Hey becomes the first person to detect radio emissions from the Sun, laying the basis for the development of radio astronomy.

FEB

	Chinese seamen in Liverpool strike for improved pay and equality of treatment with British sailors (February-April).
10th	Soap rationing is introduced across Britain.

15th February: Lieutenant-General Arthur Ernest Percival's forces surrender to the Japanese at the Battle of Singapore. Around 80,000 British, Indian and Australian troops in Singapore become prisoners of war in what is the largest surrender of British-led forces in history. *Photo: Bearing the Union Jack and a white flag, General Percival (far right), marches towards the Japanese camp to surrender Singapore to General Tomoyuki Yamashita of the Imperial Japanese Army.*

16th	Bangka Island massacre: Japanese soldiers machine-gun 22 Australian Army nurses and 60 Australian and British soldiers who had survived the sinking of Vyner Brooke by Japanese bombers; only one nurse and two soldiers survive.
19th	Clement Attlee is appointed as the first ever Deputy Prime Minister of the U.K.

MAR

3rd	The first operational mission of the Avro Lancaster bomber, deploying naval mines in the vicinity of Heligoland Bight, is performed by aircraft of No.44 Sqn. based at RAF Waddington in Lincolnshire. *NB: The first bombing mission by the Avro Lancaster was conducted over the German city of Essen 8 days later.*
28th	234 Wellington and Stirling bombers drop approximately 400 tons of bombs over the German city of Lubeck. It is the first major destructive attack of the war by RAF Bomber Command; twelve RAF aircraft are lost in the attack.

MAR

28th March: Operation Chariot: A daring amphibious attack by the Royal Navy and British Commandos is undertaken on the heavily defended Normandie dry dock at St Nazaire in German-occupied France. The obsolete destroyer HMS Campbeltown (packed with delayed-action explosives) is rammed into the Normandie dock gates whilst commandos land to destroy machinery and other structures. The operation is a major tactical success and puts the dock out of service until 1948. Of the 611 men who took part in the raid, 169 were killed (German causalities were in excess of 360). To recognise their bravery 89 men were awarded decorations including five Victoria Crosses. *Photo: HMS Campbeltown shortly before the explosion at the Normandie dry dock.*

APR

	The Women's Timber Corps is set up to work in forestry, replacing men who had left to join the armed forces. *Interesting facts: At its peak in 1943 there were some 13,000 women, commonly known as Lumber Jills, employed by the WTC. The women were paid piece-work and their pay ranged from 35 to about 50 shillings per week. The WTC was disbanded in 1946.*
1st	The Exeter-born Archbishop of York, William Temple, replaces Cosmo Gordon Lang as the Archbishop of Canterbury.
5th	The Japanese Navy attacks Colombo in Ceylon (Sri Lanka). Royal Navy Cruisers HMS Cornwall and HMS Dorsetshire are sunk southwest of the island.
9th	The Japanese Navy launches an air raid on Trincomalee in Ceylon; Royal Navy aircraft carrier HMS Hermes and Royal Australian Navy Destroyer HMAS Vampire are sunk off the country's East Coast.

15th | George VI awards the George Cross to people of Malta so as to "bear witness to the heroism and devotion of its people". *Fun fact: The George Cross was incorporated into the flag of Malta in 1943 and remains in the current design to this day.*

23rd April: Exeter becomes the first city bombed by German Luftwaffe as part of the "Baedeker Blitz" in retaliation for the British bombing of Lübeck. Whilst this particular raid caused little damage, a second raid the following night was more severe with over 80 fatalities (the Luftwaffe returned to Exeter on the 3rd - 4th May causing heavy damage to the city centre and further 164 deaths). *Photo: The bombed ruins of Southernhay West in Exeter after the Baedeker Raids in Spring 1942.*

The Baedeker Blitz was a tit-for-tat exchange by the Luftwaffe with the hope of forcing the RAF to reduce their attacks on Germany. Targets were chosen to increase the effect on civilian life, and for their cultural and historical significance, rather than for any military value. The main set of raids continued from late April until early June, although other towns and cities continued to be targeted for their cultural value over the next two years. Across all the raids in this period a total of 1,637 civilians were killed, 1,760 injured, and over 50,000 houses were destroyed. Some noted buildings were destroyed or damaged, including York's Guildhall and the Bath Assembly Rooms, but on the whole most escaped. Damage to the targeted cities was minimal compared to the German bombing campaign of 1940-1941, and the Baedeker raids are generally seen militarily as an abject failure.

APR

24th	Barnburgh Main Colliery in the Dearne Valley, South Yorkshire, suffers a collapse in the Park Gate coal seam; 4 miners are killed.

25th April: Sixteen-year-old Princess Elizabeth (the only woman in the royal family to have served in the military) registers for war service under the Ministry of Labour's Youth Registration Scheme. *Photos: Princess Elizabeth (truck mechanic No.230873) in her Auxiliary Territorial Service uniform in front of an Army ambulance during WW2 / The Princess, wearing her Girl Guides uniform, signs up for war service.*

25th	Baedeker Blitz: Three bombing raids on Bath by 80 Luftwaffe aircraft kill 417 and injure 1,000 over the weekend of 25th - 27th April.
27th	Baedeker Blitz: The Luftwaffe attack Norwich dropping more than 90 tons of bombs and causing 67 deaths; it is the most severe raid to hit the city during the war. Two nights later, on the 29th April, another raid takes place destroying many buildings in the city centre.
29th	Baedeker Blitz: Forty German bombers attack York and in less than two hours damage over 9,000 buildings in the city; 92 people are killed.

MAY

5th	Battle of Madagascar: British commander Major-General Robert Sturges of the Royal Marines leads the invasion of Vichy French-held Madagascar.
6th	The Radio Doctor (Charles Hill) makes his first BBC radio broadcast giving advice on wartime diet and how to stay healthy.
21st	The Allied Arctic Convoy PQ16 departs Hvalfjord in Iceland with aid for the Soviet Union. Of the 35 merchant ships (8 British) 25 arrived safely in Russia on the 30th May.
26th	The Anglo-Soviet Treaty (establishing a military and political alliance between the Soviet Union and the British Empire) is signed in London by British Foreign Secretary Anthony Eden and Soviet Foreign Minister Vyacheslav Molotov.
30th	Operation Millennium: The RAF dispatches 1,047 bombers to Cologne in its first "thousand bomber raid". It is the largest bombing raid of World War II.

JUN

1st	Baedeker Blitz: The Luftwaffe descend on Canterbury carpeting it with bombs in a savage act of retaliation by Hitler for the RAF's bombing of Cologne; 43 people are killed and some 800 buildings destroyed.
19th	U.S. President Franklin D. Roosevelt and British Prime Minister Winston Churchill arrive in Washington, D.C. for a conference (19th - 25th June). An agreement is reached to start preparations for an invasion of the North African Colonies of Vichy France (Operation Torch).

23rd June: German Luftwaffe pilot Armin Faber lands his Focke-Wulf FW190 (Germany's latest fighter aircraft) at RAF Pembrey in Wales. Disoriented Faber had mistaken the Bristol Channel for the English Channel and thought he was landing in France. Observers on the ground could not believe their eyes as Faber waggled his wings in a victory celebration, before lowering the Focke-Wulf's undercarriage and landing. *Follow up: Faber's plane was the first FW190 to be captured by the Allies and this allowed it to be tested to reveal any weaknesses that could be exploited. Photo: Faber's captured Focke Wulf at the Royal Aircraft Establishment, Farnborough, with the RAE's chief test pilot, Wing Commander H J "Willie" Wilson at the controls (August 1942).*

JUL

	On the Scottish island of Gruinard military scientists begin the testing of anthrax as a biological warfare agent.
7th	John Maynard Keynes, one of the most influential economists of the 20th century, takes his seat in the British House of Lords as Baron Keynes of Tilton after receiving an hereditary peerage in the King's Birthday Honours.
10th	The patriotic Academy Award-winning drama film Mrs. Miniver, starring Greer Garson, is released in London. *Fun facts: Set rural England it becomes the first film to receive five acting nominations at the Academy Awards.*
26th	The rationing of sweets and chocolate is introduced. The new rules give an allowance of 8oz (227g) per month to everyone over five years of age.

4th	British premier Winston Churchill arrives in Cairo. Whilst in Egypt he takes the decision to relieve Claude Auckinleck as Commander-in-Chief of the Middle East Theatre.
8th	Lieutenant-General Bernard Montgomery is appointed commander of the British Eighth Army in North Africa.
11th	The British aircraft carrier HMS Eagle is torpedoed by the German submarine U-73 and sinks within four minutes; 131 officers and ratings, mainly from the ship's propulsion machinery spaces, are killed; 67 officers and 862 sailors are rescued.
11th	Traffic is admitted onto the new Waterloo Bridge across the Thames in London. *Notes: Although partially opened on Tuesday 11th March 1942, the bridge was not fully completed until 1945.*
12th	Prime Minister Winston Churchill arrives in Moscow for a conference with Joseph Stalin and U.S. representative W. Averrell Harriman.
19th	British and Canadian troops conduct the Dieppe Raid (Operation Jubilee), an amphibious attack on the German-occupied port of Dieppe in northern France. Aerial and naval support is insufficient to enable the ground forces to achieve their objectives and within ten hours, of the 6,086 men who landed, 3,623 had been killed, wounded or become prisoners of war. The RAF lost 106 aircraft and the Royal Navy lost 33 landing craft and a destroyer. *Follow up: The lessons of the Dieppe Raid influenced preparations for Allied seaborne operations in the Mediterranean and the Normandy landings (Operation Overlord).*

25th August: Prince George, Duke of Kent, brother of George VI, is among 14 killed in a military air crash near Dunbeath in the Scottish Highlands. *NB: A Royal Air Force Board of Inquiry later determines that the crash is the result of a navigational error by the crew.*

30th	Battle of Alam el Halfa: General Montgomery leads the Eighth Army to victory over Field Marshal Rommel's Afrika Korps in Egypt (30th August - 5th September).

SEP

10th	Three hundred and sixty RAF aircraft drop 700 tons of bombs on Dusseldorf.
11th	Hodder & Stoughton publish Enid Blyton's "Five on a Treasure Island". It is the first of her Famous Five children's novels and the start of one of the best-selling children's series ever with over 100 million books sold to date.
12th	The British transport ship RMS Laconia is torpedoed and sunk by German submarine U-156 in the Atlantic, 130 miles north of Ascension Island, with the loss of around 2,000 lives, mainly Italian prisoners of war.
17th	Noël Coward's patriotic war film In Which We Serve premieres. *Note: The film received the full backing of the Ministry of Information which offered advice on what would make good propaganda, and also facilitated the release of military personnel.*

OCT

2nd	The Royal Navy's First World War cruiser HMS Curaçao is accidentally sliced in half and sunk by the ocean liner troop ship RMS Queen Mary off the coast of Donegal; 337 officers and men of her crew are lost.
2nd	The Japanese troopship Lisbon Maru sinks following a torpedo attack the previous day by United States Navy submarine USS Grouper off the coast of China: 829 are killed, mostly British prisoners of war who (unknown to the attacker) are being held on board.
5th	Oxfam: The first meeting of the Oxford Committee for Famine Relief (founded by a group of Quakers, social activists and Oxford academics) is held in the Old Library, the University Church, Oxford.
9th	The Statute of Westminster Adoption Act is passed by the Parliament of Australia formalising Australian autonomy from the United Kingdom.
23rd	British and Commonwealth forces launch a major attack against German and Italian forces in the Second Battle of El Alamein in Egypt.
29th	A public meeting at the Royal Albert Hall in London, presided over by the Archbishop of Canterbury and with international political figures in attendance, registers its outrage over the persecution of Jews by Nazi Germany. Churchill sends a message to the meeting stating that "Free men and women denounce these vile crimes, and when this world struggle ends with the enthronement of human rights, racial persecution will be ended".
30th	British sailors Lieutenant Anthony Fasson, Able Seaman Colin Grazier and NAAFI canteen assistant Tommy Brown, board the German submarine U-559 as it sinks in the Mediterranean and retrieve the U-boat's Enigma key setting sheets with all current settings for the U-boat Enigma network. The code-book material they retrieved was immensely valuable to the code-breakers at Bletchley Park and this captured material allowed them to read the cyphers for several weeks, and to break U-boat Enigma thereafter right through to the end of the war.

NOV

8th	British and American troops, commanded by General Dwight D. Eisenhower, invade French North Africa in Operation Torch. It is the first mass involvement of U.S. troops in the European-North African Theatre, and sees the first major airborne assault carried out by the United States.

11th November: Second Battle of El Alamein: Field Marshal Erwin Rommel is comprehensively defeated by the British Eighth Army under the command of Lieutenant-General Bernard Montgomery. The Allied victory is the beginning of the end of the Western Desert Campaign, eliminating the Axis threat to Egypt, the Suez Canal and the Middle Eastern and Persian oil fields. *Photos: Montgomery in the turret of his Grant command tank at El Alamein / British troops unloading fuel drums at El-Alamein during the North Africa campaigns.*

17th	Admiral Max Horton takes over from Percy Noble as Commander-in-Chief, Western Approaches, with responsibility for the safety of Atlantic convoys.
26th	The first operational military Bailey bridge is erected by British Royal Engineers (237 Field Company) over the Medjerda River near Medjez el Bab in Tunisia. *Interesting facts: Invented by Donald Bailey (a civil servant in the British War Office), by the end of the war the U.S. Fifth Army and British Eighth Army had built over 3,000 Bailey bridges in Sicily and Italy alone.*

DEC

2nd	The government publishes the Beveridge Report. Drafted by the Liberal economist William Beveridge it proposes widespread reforms to the system of social welfare to address what Beveridge identified as "five giants on the road of reconstruction": "Want... Disease, Ignorance, Squalor and Idleness". *NB: Overwhelmingly popular with the public, it formed the basis for many post-war reforms such as the expansion of National Insurance and the creation of the National Health Service.*
7th	Operation Frankton: Ten British Royal Marines conduct a daring raid on ships in Bordeaux harbour. Launched from a submarine in the Gironde estuary they paddled by night to Bordeaux into canoes loaded with limpet mines. The raid saw six ships in the harbour damaged. *Note: A heavily fictionalised version of the story was depicted in the film The Cockleshell Heroes (1955).*
31st	The Battle of the Barents Sea takes place between warships of the German Navy (Kriegsmarine) and British ships escorting convoy JW 51B to Kola Inlet in the USSR. *Note: The German raiders' failure to inflict significant losses on the convoy infuriated Hitler who ordered that German naval strategy would henceforth concentrate on the U-boat fleet rather than surface ships.*

Worldwide News & Events

1. 1st January: Representatives of 26 countries fighting the Rome-Berlin-Tokyo Axis decide to affirm their support by signing the Declaration of The United Nations. *Notes: President Roosevelt, Prime Minister Churchill, Maxim Litvinov of the USSR and T.V. Soong of China signed the short document on New Year's Day, followed on the 2nd January by the representatives of twenty-two other nations. The declaration pledged the signatory governments to the maximum war effort and bound them against making a separate peace.*

2. 6th January: Pan American Airlines becomes the first commercial airline to schedule a flight around the world. The "Pacific Clipper", a Boeing 314 Clipper flying boat, completed its circumnavigation of the world when it landed at LaGuardia Field seaplane base in New York City after departing San Francisco on the 2nd December 1941. *NB: One of the largest aircraft of its time, just twelve Boeing 314 Clippers were built, nine of which served with Pan Am*

3. 7th January: United States and Philippine troops, under the command of General Douglas MacArthur, engage the Japanese in the Battle of Bataan. The battle lasts until the 9th April and represents the most intense phase of the Japanese invasion of the Philippines during World War II.

4. 9th January: In his 20th title defence Joe Louis KOs Buddy Baer in the 1st round of their rematch to retain his world heavyweight boxing titles at New York's Madison Square Garden (raising $47,000 for the Navy Relief Society). The next day he volunteers to enlist as a private in the U.S. Army at Camp Upton on Long Island, New York. *Fun facts: In all Louis made 25 defences of his heavyweight titles between 1937 and 1948, and was world champion for 11 years and 10 months. His most remarkable record is that he knocked out 23 opponents in 27 title fights, including five world champions. Photos: Private Louis at Fort Dix, New Jersey (1942) / Joe Louis (1946).*

5. 11th January: The Japanese conquer Kuala Lumpur in Malaya. They encounter very little resistance; British troops had already left the city.

6. | 13th January: German test pilot Helmut Schenk becomes the first person to escape from a stricken aircraft using an ejector seat after his control surfaces ice up and become inoperative.

7. | 13th January: Henry Ford patents a method for constructing car body parts made out of plastic formed from soybeans. *Follow up: The plastic Ford was never made due to World War II and car production being halted across the United States.*

8. | 14th January: Operation Drumbeat: The German submarine U-123, under the command of Reinhard Hardegen, sinks the 9,500-ton Norwegian tanker Norness within sight of Long Island, New York. No warships are dispatched to investigate and over the following nights U-123 is presented with a succession of easy targets including (the following night) the 6,700-ton British tanker Coimbra off Sandy Hook. *Notes: During the war U-123 conducted 12 war patrols, sinking 45 ships totalling 227,174-tons and damaging six others totalling 53,568-tons.*

9. | 16th January: Actress Carole Lombard is among 22 killed aboard TWA Flight-3 after it crashes into Potosi Mountain near Las Vegas, Nevada. *NB: Lombard had been returning from a War Bond rally and had raised more than $2 million in defence bonds in a single evening. The crash was attributed to the flight crew's inability to properly navigate the mountains surrounding Las Vegas.*

10. | 20th January: Senior Nazi government officials and Schutzstaffel (SS) leaders hold the notorious Wannsee Conference in Berlin to organise the 'Final Solution to the Jewish Question', the rounding up and extermination of Europe's Jews.

11. | 27th January: A record low of -27.4°C is recorded by Jaap Langedijk in Dutch town of Winterswijk; it is the coldest day in the Netherlands since 1850.

12. | 1st February: Vidkun Quisling is elected to the post of Minister-President of the Norwegian national government. *Follow up: Quisling, a Nazi collaborator, was executed by firing squad in Oslo on the 24th October 1945 after being found guilty of charges including embezzlement, murder and high treason against the Norwegian state. The word "quisling" is now more commonly known for; a person who collaborates with an enemy occupying force, a traitor.*

13. 9th February: The seized ocean liner SS Normandie catches fire while being converted into the troopship USS Lafayette at pier 88 in New York City; hours later she capsizes. *Follow up: Although the French built ocean liner was later salvaged at great expense, restoration was deemed too costly and she was scrapped on the 3rd October 1946. Photo: A Coast Guard aircraft flies over the wreck of Lafayette (c. 1943).*

14. 9th February: The Combined Chiefs of Staff (the supreme military staff for the United States and Britain during World War II) holds its first formal meeting to coordinate U.S. military operations between War and Navy Departments.

15. 10th February: The record label RCA Victor presents Glenn Miller with the first ever gold record for selling a million copies of his hit recording "Chattanooga Choo Choo". The song, about a train ride from New York to Chattanooga in Tennessee, was recorded on the 7th May 1941, and when released had become an immediate success. *Fun fact: The 1941 recording of "Chattanooga Choo Choo" by Glenn Miller and His Orchestra was inducted into the Grammy Hall of Fame in 1996.*

16. 14th February: The Polish resistance movement, the Home Army, is formed. *Note: It will eventually become the largest resistance movement in occupied Europe.*

17. 19th February: America's President Franklin D. Roosevelt signs Executive Order 9066 authorising military commanders to designate "military areas" at their discretion "from which any or all persons may be excluded". *Follow up: These zones would result in the forced relocation and incarceration in concentration camps of thousands of people of Japanese, German and Italian ancestry, many of whom are American citizens.*

18. 19th February: In the largest single attack ever mounted by a foreign power on Australia, the Japanese launch 242 warplanes (in two separate raids) attacking the city of Darwin.

19. 20th February: Lieutenant Edward O'Hare becomes America's first WWII flying ace after he single-handedly attacks a formation of nine Japanese bombers (shooting down five) approaching his aircraft carrier. *Note: In 1949 the O'Hare International Airport near Chicago was named in his honour (now the world's sixth-busiest airport).*

20. 26th February: The 14th Academy Awards ceremony, honouring the best in film for 1941, is held at the Biltmore Hotel in Los Angeles. The Oscar winners include John Ford's film How Green Was My Valley, Gary Cooper and Joan Fontaine. *Photo: Gary Cooper, Joan Fontaine, and best supporting actors, Mary Astor and Donald Crisp.*

21.	27th February: Battle of Java Sea: Allied navies suffer a disastrous defeat over a period of three days at the hands of the Imperial Japanese Navy. The defeat leads to the Japanese occupation of the entire Dutch East Indies.
22.	5th March: The world premiere of Dmitri Shostakovich's 7th Symphony takes place in Kuybyshev (now Samara), Russia. *Notes: The work is regarded as a major musical testament to the 27 million Soviet people who lost their lives in World War II, and it is often played at Leningrad Cemetery where half a million victims of the 900-day Siege of Leningrad are buried.*
23.	11th March: President Roosevelt orders General Douglas MacArthur to leave the Philippine island of Corregidor to go to Australia as American defence of the island (surrounded by the Japanese) collapses. He arrives in Melbourne six days later where he is formally appointed supreme commander of the South-West Pacific Area.
24.	17th March: The Nazi extermination camp Bełżec begins the systematic gassing of Jews. *NB: Between 430,000 and 500,000 Jews are believed to have been murdered by the SS at Bełżec, making it the third-deadliest Nazi extermination camp exceeded only by Treblinka and Auschwitz.*
25.	27th March: The first transport of French Jews to Auschwitz by Nazi-Germany takes place. *NB: Of the 75,721 deportees from France to Nazi extermination camps only 2,560 survived through to 1945.*
26.	27th March: In his 21st title defence (a military charity bout) Joe Louis KOs Abe Simon in the 6th round to retain his world heavyweight boxing titles at New York's Madison Square Garden; the fight nets $36,146.
27.	9th April: After a three month fight American and Filipino forces surrender to the Japanese at Bataan. *Note: The surrender of the 76,000 troops at Bataan is the largest in United States military history since the American Civil War's Battle of Harper's Ferry.*
28.	26th April: A gas and coal-dust explosion kills 1,549 at the Honkeiko colliery in Liaoning, China (then part of the Japanese-controlled puppet state of Manchukuo). Although some workers are killed by the explosion an investigation after the war by the Soviet Union found that most deaths were from carbon monoxide poisoning (produced when the Japanese shut off the ventilation and sealed the pit in an attempt to curtail the fire). *Note: The Honkeiko colliery disaster is the worst in the history of coal mining.*
29.	29th April: Jewish Dutch people are ordered to wear yellow badges by the German authorities; Belgian Jews and Jews in occupied France are ordered to do the same on the 3rd June and 7th June respectively.
30.	4th May: The Battle of Coral Sea begins. *NB: The battle is historically significant as the first naval battle fought solely in the air (between the Imperial Japanese Navy and naval and air forces of the United States and Australia).*
31.	4th May: The Pulitzer Prize for the Novel (now the Pulitzer Prize for Fiction) is awarded to Ellen Glasgow for In This Our Life.
32.	5th May: Sugar becomes the first consumer commodity rationed in United States; people are limited to ½ pound (227g) per person per week.
33.	6th May: In the Philippines the Battle of Corregidor ends as the last American and Filipino forces surrender to the Japanese.
34.	12th May: David Ben-Gurion assembles an emergency conference of American Zionists in New York City; the convention decides upon the establishment of a Jewish commonwealth in Palestine after the war. *Notes: The State of Israel was established on the 14th May 1948 with Ben-Gurion its primary national founder and first Prime Minister.*

35.	22nd May: Mexican President Manuel Ávila Camacho issues a formal declaration of war against the Axis Powers after the sinking of two Mexican oil tankers by German U-boats.
36.	27th May: Nazi leader Reinhard Heydrich (one of the most powerful men in Nazi Germany and an important figure in the rise of Adolf Hitler) is mortally wounded by a grenade thrown by Czech rebels in Prague during Operation Anthropoid; he dies a week later (4th June).
37.	29th May: Bing Crosby records White Christmas for Decca Records with the John Scott Trotter Orchestra and the Ken Darby Singers. *Fun facts: Written by Irving Berlin for the musical film Holiday Inn (1942), White Christmas is the world's best-selling single of all time with estimated sales in excess of 50 million copies worldwide. The composition also notably won the Academy Award for Best Original Song at the 15th Academy Awards on the 4th March 1943.*

38. 4th - 7th June: Battle of Midway: Six months after Japan's attack on Pearl Harbor and one month after the Battle of the Coral Sea, the U.S. Navy, under Admirals Chester W. Nimitz, Frank J. Fletcher, and Raymond A. Spruance, defeat an attacking fleet of the Imperial Japanese Navy near Midway Atoll. The devastating damage inflicted during the battle (which renders the Japanese aircraft carriers irreparable) has been described as the most stunning and decisive blow in the history of naval warfare. *Photo: Smoke pours from USS Yorktown after being hit by Japanese dive bombers at Midway (4th June); the Yorktown is eventually sunk after being hit by a salvo of torpedoes fired from the Japanese submarine I-168 on the 7th June.*

39.	5th June: The U.S. Congress declares war on Bulgaria, Hungary and Romania.
40.	12th June: In Amsterdam Anne Frank gets a diary for her 13th birthday; she begins writing in it two days later. *Notes: Published posthumously (she is believed to have died of typhus in the Bergen-Belsen concentration camp in February or March 1945) the "The Diary of a Young Girl" has received widespread critical and popular attention and been translated into over 70 languages.*
41.	18th June: Eric Nessler of France stays aloft in a glider for a record 38h:21m:24s over the Montagne Noire, in the Haute-Garonne, France.
42.	21st June: The highest temperature ever recorded in Asia, 54°C (129°F), is set at Tirat Zvi in Israel.

43.	21st June: The Axis forces, led by Generalleutnant Erwin Rommel, take Tobruk in North Africa.
44.	25th June: Dwight Eisenhower is appointed commander of U.S. forces in Europe.
45.	30th June: For the second month in a row U-boats sink and damage 146 allied ships; these are the highest monthly totals recorded during WWII (May - 146 ships, 722,666-tons / June - 146 ships, 700,227-tons).
46.	4th July: The U.S. Eighth Air Force flies its first inauspicious mission in Europe using borrowed British planes to attack the Dutch Alkmaar, Hammsted, and Valkenburg airfields; of the six aircraft that went out only three make it back.
47.	18th July: The Messerschmitt Me 262 makes its first flight under jet power in Leipheim near Günzburg, Germany. Flown by test pilot Fritz Wendel, it is the world's first operational jet-powered fighter aircraft.
48.	22nd July: Over a period of eight weeks Warsaw Ghetto inmates are shuttled by train to the Treblinka extermination camp. The operation, led by SS-Sturmbannführer Hermann Höfle, sees the murder of 254,000 Jews at the camp between the 23rd July and 21st September.
49.	7th August: The Battle of Guadalcanal, the first major land offensive by Allied forces against the Empire of Japan, begins (ends the 9th February 1943). *NB: The Guadalcanal campaign is widely considered, along with the Battle of Midway, a turning point in the Pacific War.*
50.	9th August: British officials imprison Mahatma Gandhi hoping to suppress a civil disobedience program intended to free India from colonial rule.
51.	13th August: The Manhattan Project is officially created under the direction of Major General Leslie Groves of the U.S. Army Corps of Engineers (its aim is to deliver an atomic bomb).
52.	15th August: Operation Pedestal: The American tanker SS Ohio reaches Malta as part of a British operation to carry vital supplies to the island.
53.	17th August: Eighth Air Force bombers (escorted by British RAF Spitfires) bomb the Sotteville railyard 3 miles South of Rouen, France. It is the "first combat action" of the Eighth Air Force, and the first B-17 bombing of Europe.
54.	22nd August: Brazil, under the dictatorship of Getúlio Vargas, declares war on Germany, Japan and Italy.
55.	23rd August: The Battle of Stalingrad: Germany and its allies begin their fight against the Soviet Union for control of the city of Stalingrad (now Volgograd) in Southern Russia. *Follow up: The battle, marked by fierce close-quarters combat and direct assaults on civilians in air raids, is one of the bloodiest battles in the history of warfare with an estimated 2 million casualties. The Axis forces, having exhausted their ammunition and food, surrendered on the 2nd February 1943.*
56.	20th September: Swedish runner Gunther Hagg sets a world record time in the 5000m (13m:58.2s) to become the World Record Holder at all distances from 1500m to 5000m.
57.	3rd October: The first V-2 rocket is successfully launched from Test Stand VII at Peenemünde in Germany; it flies a distance of 91.3 miles (147km) and reaches a height of 52.5 miles (84.5km). *Interesting facts: The V-2 rocket became the first artificial object to travel into space when crossing the Kármán line (measured at 62 miles (100km) above Earth's mean sea level) on the 20th June 1944.*
58.	16th October: A Cyclone in Bay of Bengal, India, near the West Bengal / Odisha border, kills some 15,000 people.
59.	23rd October: American Airlines Flight 28 is struck by an U.S. Army Air Force bomber near Palm Springs, California. Amongst the victims is the award-winning composer and Hollywood songwriter Ralph Rainger (Academy Award for Best Original Song 1938 - "Thanks for the Memory").

VIEW ALONG THE NEW ALASKA HIGHWAY THROUGH CANADA'S WILDERNESS
BUILT BY A WELCOME ARMY OF U. S. SOLDIERS
PERMISSION WARTIME INFORMATION BOARD

60. 28th October: The Alaska Highway is completed with the northern linkup at Mile 1202, Beaver Creek. *Interesting facts: The Alaska Highway was built by 10,000 men of the U.S. Army Corps of Engineers as a supply route. Although completed in 1942 it was not usable by general vehicles until 1943, and wasn't opened to the public until 1948. Photo: Postcard of Suicide Hill on the Alcan Highway, Mile 148 (c. 1942).*

61. 6th November: The German Luftwaffe Heinkel He 219 night fighter aircraft makes its first flight; it is the first operational military aircraft to be equipped with an ejector seat.

62. 7th November: Cyclist Fausto Coppi establishes a new world hour record of 45.798km/h in Milan, Italy.

63. 23rd November: Chinese sailor Poon Lim, working as second steward on the British merchant ship SS Benlomond, jumps overboard after the Benlomond is hit by torpedoes from German submarine U-172. The sole survivor, he finds an eight-foot wooden raft and begins what will be 133 days adrift in the South Atlantic. *Follow up: Lin was rescued by three fishermen as he neared the coast of Brazil on the 5th April 1943. After four weeks in a Brazilian hospital the British Consul arranged for him to return to Britain. Upon his return Lin was awarded a British Empire Medal by King George VI.*

64. 26th November: The movie Casablanca, starring Humphrey Bogart and Ingrid Bergman, premieres at the Hollywood Theatre in New York City (Academy Awards Best Picture 1943).

65. 28th November: A fire at the Cocoanut Grove nightclub in Boston, Massachusetts, kills 492 people. *NB: The fire (the deadliest nightclub fire in history) leads to a reform of safety standards and codes across America.*

66. 2nd December: A team led by Enrico Fermi initiates the world's first self-sustaining nuclear chain reaction at the University of Chicago.

67. 10th December: An official diplomatic note from the government of Poland in exile, regarding the extermination of Jews in German-occupied Poland, is sent to the foreign ministers of the Allies. It is the first official report on the Holocaust.

68. 19th December: Robert Stroud (the Birdman of Alcatraz) is transferred to Alcatraz Federal Penitentiary in San Francisco Bay (inmate No.594).

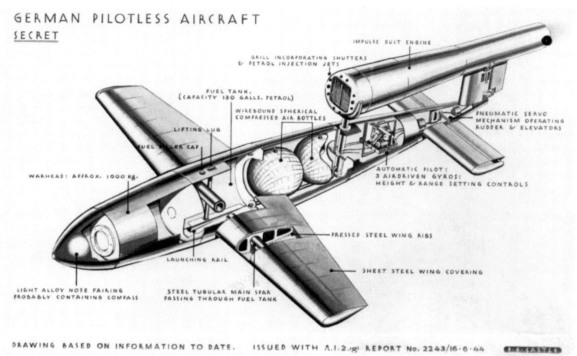

GERMAN PILOTLESS AIRCRAFT
SECRET

DRAWING BASED ON INFORMATION TO DATE.   ISSUED WITH A.I.2.(g) REPORT No. 2243/16-6-44

69. 24th December: The first powered flight of the V-1 flying bomb (aka; buzz bomb or doodlebug) takes place at Peenemunde in Germany. *Notes: An early cruise missile and the only production aircraft to use a pulsejet for power, the V-1 was the first of the so-called "Vengeance weapons" series (Vergeltungswaffen) deployed for the terror bombing of London.*

70. 28th December: Captain Robert Sullivan, flying from New York to Portugal, becomes the first pilot to fly across the Atlantic 100 times.

BIRTHS

British Personalities

BORN IN 1942

John Thaw, CBE
b. 3rd January 1942
d. 21st February 2002
Television, stage and film actor.

Jan Leeming
b. 5th January 1942

Television presenter and newsreader.

Stephen Hawking, CH, CBE, FRS, FRSA
b. 8th January 1942
d. 14th March 2018
Theoretical physicist, cosmologist and
author.

Michael Crawford, CBE
b. 19th January 1942

Actor, comedian and singer.

Terry Jones

b. 1st February 1942
d. 21st January 2020

Actor, writer, comedian, screenwriter, film director and historian.

Graham Nash, OBE

b. 2nd February 1942

British-American singer-songwriter and musician (Hollies / Crosby, Stills & Nash).

Brian Jones

b. 28th February 1942
d. 3rd July 1969

Musician and composer (Rolling Stones).

John Cale, OBE

b. 9th March 1942

Musician, composer, singer, songwriter and record producer (Velvet Underground).

Geoffrey Hayes

b. 13th March 1942
d. 30th September 2018

Television presenter and actor best known as the presenter of Rainbow.

Richard O'Brien

b. 25th March 1942

English-New Zealand actor, writer, musician and television presenter.

Michael York, OBE
b. 27th March 1942

Actor who has appeared in over 70 films.

Lord **Neil Kinnock**, PC
b. 28th March 1942

Politician and former Leader of the Labour
Party / Opposition (1983-1992).

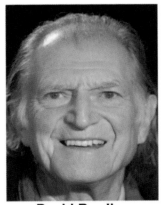

David Bradley
b. 17th April 1942

Television, film and stage actor.

Lord **Norman Lamont**, PC
b. 8th May 1942

Conservative politician and former
Chancellor of the Exchequer (1990-1993).

Ian Dury
b. 12th May 1942
d. 27th March 2000
Singer-songwriter and actor.

Nobby Stiles, MBE
b. 18th May 1942
d. 30th October 2020
World Cup winning footballer and manager.

Sir **Fraser Stoddart**, FRS, FRSE, FRSC
b. 24th May 1942

Chemist and joint winner of the Nobel Prize
in Chemistry (2016).

Fred Dinenage, MBE
b. 8th June 1942

Television presenter, broadcaster and
author.

Ossie Clark
b. 9th June 1942
d. 6th August 1996
Fashion designer who was a major figure in
the Swinging Sixties scene in London.

Gordon Burns
b. 10th June 1942

Northern Irish game show host, journalist
and broadcaster.

Sir **Paul McCartney**, CH, MBE
b. 18th June 1942

Singer, songwriter, musician, and record
and film producer.

Dustin Gee
b. 24th June 1942
d. 3rd January 1986
Impressionist and comedian best known for
his double act with Les Dennis.

Prince Michael of Kent, GCVO, CD
b. 4th July 1942

Member of the Royal Family (grandson of
King George V and Queen Mary).

Peter Sissons
b. 17th July 1942
d. 1st October 2019
Journalist and broadcaster.

Judith Keppel
b. 18th August 1942

Quiz show contestant who won a million
pounds on Who Wants to Be a Millionaire?

Gerry Marsden, MBE
b. 24th September 1942
d. 3rd January 2021
Singer-songwriter, musician and television
personality (Gerry and the Pacemakers).

Mike Berry
b. 24th September 1942

Singer and actor.

Bernard Jewry
b. 27th September 1942
d. 23rd October 2014
Rock singer and stage actor (aka Shane
Fenton / Alvin Stardust).

Dame Anita Roddick, DBE
b. 23rd October 1942
d. 10th September 2007
Businesswoman (The Body Shop), and
environmental and human rights activist.

Bob Hoskins
b. 26th October 1942
d. 29th April 2014
Actor.

Jean Shrimpton
b. 7th November 1942

Model and actress, considered to be one of
the world's first supermodels.

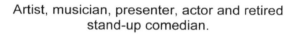

Sir Billy Connolly, CBE
b. 24th November 1942

Artist, musician, presenter, actor and retired
stand-up comedian.

Gemma Jones
b. 4th December 1942

Actress on both stage and screen.

Andy Summers
b. 31st December 1942

Guitarist who was a member of the rock
band the Police.

Notable British Deaths

16th Jan	Prince Arthur, Duke of Connaught and Strathearn (b. 1st May 1850) - The seventh child of Queen Victoria and Prince Albert. Arthur served as the tenth Governor General of Canada between 1911 and 1916.
22nd Jan	Walter Richard Sickert, RA, RBA (b. 31st May 1860) - Painter and printmaker who was a member of the Camden Town Group of Post-Impressionist artists in early 20th century London.
26th Feb	William Waldegrave Palmer, 2nd Earl of Selborne, KG, GCMG, PC (b. 17th October 1859) - Politician and colonial administrator who served as High Commissioner for Southern Africa.
3rd Mar	The Very Reverend Sir George Adam Smith, FRSE, FBA (b. 19th October 1856) - Scottish theologian who was appointed a Chaplain-in-Ordinary to King George V in 1933, and reappointed by King Edward VIII and King George VI.
12th Mar	Sir William Henry Bragg, OM, KBE, PRS (b. 2nd July 1862) - Physicist, chemist, mathematician and active sportsman who uniquely shared the 1915 Nobel Prize in Physics with his son Lawrence Bragg. The mineral Braggite is named after him and his son.
15th Mar	Arthur Heygate Mackmurdo (b. 12th December 1851) - Progressive architect and designer who influenced the Arts and Crafts movement, notably through the Century Guild of Artists which he set up in partnership with Herbert Horne in 1882.
27th Mar	Major General Sir Vernon George Waldegrave Kell, KCMG, KBE, CB (b. 21st November 1873) - Army general and the founder and first Director of the British Security Service (otherwise known as MI5).
17th Apr	Laura Annie Willson, MBE (b. 15th August 1877) - Engineer and suffragette who was twice imprisoned for her political activities. She was one of the founding members of the Women's Engineering Society and was the first female member of the Federation of House Builders.
17th May	Alfred Hollins (b. 11th September 1865) - Organist, composer and teacher who was noted as a recitalist in Scotland.
23rd May	Charles Robert Ashbee (b. 17th May 1863) - Architect and designer who was a prime mover of the Arts and Crafts movement.
7th Jun	Alan Dower Blumlein (b. 29th June 1903) - Electronics engineer, notable for his many inventions in telecommunications, sound recording, stereophonic sound, television and radar.
10th Jun	Stanley Richard Lupino Hook (b. 15th June 1893) - Actor, dancer, singer, librettist, director and short story writer known professionally as Stanley Lupino.
18th Jun	Sutherland Macdonald (b. 25th June 1860) - Tattoo artist considered to be the first person to offer a professional tattoo service in Britain.
18th Jul	George Alexander Sutherland (b. 25th March 1862) - English-born jurist and politician who served as an Associate Justice of the United States Supreme Court between 1922 and 1938.
22nd Jul	Gilbert Cunningham Joyce (b. 7th April 1866) - University educator and Bishop of Monmouth (1928-1940).
23rd Jul	Andrew Ducat (b. 16th February 1886) - Sportsman who played both cricket and football for England.

28th July: Sir William Matthew Flinders Petrie, FRS, FBA (b. 3rd June 1853) - Egyptologist who held the first chair of Egyptology in the United Kingdom and excavated many of the most important archaeological sites in Egypt (in conjunction with his wife Hilda).

Petrie was a pioneer of systematic methodology in archaeology and the preservation of artefacts. He also developed the system of dating layers based on pottery and ceramic findings.

31st Jul	Lieutenant Colonel Sir Francis Edward Younghusband, KCSI KCIE (b. 31st May 1863) - British Army officer, explorer and spiritual writer best remembered for his travels in the Far East and Central Asia. Younghusband held positions including British commissioner to Tibet and President of the Royal Geographical Society.
7th Aug	Lieutenant-General William Henry Ewart Gott, CB, CBE, DSO & Bar, MC (b. 13th August 1897) - Senior Army officer who fought during both World War I and World War II. In August 1942 he was appointed as successor to General Claude Auchinleck as commander of the Eighth Army. On the way to take up his command he was killed when his plane was shot down; his death led to the appointment of Lieutenant-General Bernard Montgomery in his place.
25th Aug	Prince George, Duke of Kent, KG, KT, GCMG, GCVO (b. 20th December 1902) - The fourth son of King George V and Queen Mary, George was the younger brother of Edward VIII and George VI.

15th October: Dame Mary Susan Etherington, DBE (b. 15th July 1864) - Singer and actress known professionally as Marie Tempest. During a career spanning 55 years she was hailed as the "queen of her profession" and was instrumental in the founding of the actors' union Equity in Britain.

Tempest was the most famous soprano in late Victorian light opera and Edwardian musical comedies. She toured extensively visiting America, Canada, Australia, New Zealand, South Africa, India, Singapore, China, Japan and the Philippines.

23rd Oct	Arthur Dolphin (b. 24th December 1885) - First-class cricketer who kept wicket for Yorkshire County Cricket Club between 1905 and 1927. After retiring as a player, Dolphin became an umpire for a decade and officiated in six Tests.
25th Oct	Edward George Arnold (b. 7th November 1876) - Cricketer who played ten Test Matches for England between 1903 and 1907, and most of his 343 first-class matches for Worcestershire between 1899 and 1913.
4th Dec	Wing Commander Hugh Gordon Malcolm, VC (b. 2nd May 1917) - Scottish airman who was awarded the Victoria Cross for valour after facing an attack by an overwhelming force of enemy fighters in North Africa.
22nd Dec	Lieutenant Elias Henry Jones (b. 21st September 1883) - A Welsh officer in the Indian Army who, together with Australian C. W. Hill, escaped from the Yozgad prisoner of war camp in Turkey during the First World War. Their story was told in Jones' book The Road to En-dor.

POPULAR MUSIC

Bing Crosby	No.1	White Christmas
Vera Lynn	No.2	The White Cliffs Of Dover
Hutch	No.3	Jealousy
Vera Lynn	No.4	How Green Was My Valley
Joe Loss & His Orchestra	No.5	Anniversary Waltz
Billy Cotton & His Band	No.6	What More Can I Say?
Bing Crosby	No.7	Moonlight Becomes You
Bert Ambrose & His Orchestra	No.8	The Sailor With The Navy Blue Eyes
Glenn Miller	No.9	Moonlight Cocktail
The Andrews Sisters	No.10	Pennsylvania Polka

NB: During this era the success of a song was tied to the sales of sheet music so a popular song would often be perfomed by many different combinations of singers and bands. The contemporary charts would often list the song without clarifying whose version was the major hit. With this in mind although the above chart has been compiled with best intent it does remain subjective.

Bing Crosby
White Christmas

Label:	Written by:	Length:
Decca	Irving Berlin	3 mins 3 secs

Harry Lillis "Bing" Crosby, Jr. (b. 3rd May 1903 - d. 14th October 1977) was a singer, comedian and an Oscar winning actor who also bred racehorses and co-owned the Pittsburgh Pirates baseball team. His trademark warm bass-baritone voice made him the best-selling recording artist of the 20th century; Crosby sold over one billion records, tapes, compact discs and digital downloads around the world.

Vera Lynn
The White Cliffs of Dover

Label:	Written by:	Length:
Decca	Burton / Kent	3 mins 18 secs

Dame **Vera Margaret Lynn**, CH, DBE, OStJ (née Welch; b. 20th March 1917 - d. 18th June 2020) was a singer, songwriter and actress whose musical recordings and performances were enormously popular during World War II. Widely known as the Forces' Sweetheart, during the war she toured Egypt, India and Burma as part of ENSA, giving outdoor concerts for the troops. "(There'll Be Bluebirds Over) The White Cliffs of Dover" was one of Lynn's best-known recordings and among the most popular World War II tunes.

Hutch
Jealousy

Label:	Written by:	Length:
HMV	May / Gade	3 mins 27 secs

Leslie Hutchinson (b. 7th March 1900 - d. 18th August 1969) was a Grenada-born singer and musician known as "Hutch". He was one of the biggest cabaret stars in the world during the 1920s and 1930s and was, for a time, the highest paid star in Europe. Hutch was one of the first stars in Britain to volunteer to entertain the troops at home and abroad during World War II, but received no formal recognition for his service.

Vera Lynn
How Green Was My Valley

Label:	Written by:	Length:
Decca	Silver / Davis	3 mins 22 secs

Vera Lynn is the oldest person to have had a No.1 album in the British charts (aged 92), and became the first centenarian to have a charting album with "Vera Lynn 100" (2017).

Joe Loss & His Orchestra
Anniversary Waltz

Label:	Written by:	Length:
HMV	Dubin / Franklin	2 mins 34 secs

Joshua Alexander "Joe" Loss, LVO, OBE (b. 22nd June 1909 - d. 6th June 1990) was a British dance band leader and musician who founded his own eponymous orchestra. The Joe Loss Orchestra was one of the most successful acts of the big band era in the 1940s, and celebrated its 85th anniversary in 2015 under the direction of vocalist Todd Miller.

Billy Cotton & His Band
What More Can I Say?

Label:	Written by:	Length:
Rex	Art Noel	2 mins 56 secs

William Edward "Billy" Cotton (b. 6th May 1899 - d. 25th March 1969) was a band leader, entertainer, accomplished racing driver and amateur footballer whose musical career began in the 1920s. One of the few whose orchestras survived the British dance band era, Cotton is now mainly remembered as a 1950s and 1960s radio and television personality (the BBC's Billy Cotton Band Show ran from 1949 to 1968 on radio, and from 1957 on television).

Bing Crosby
Moonlight Becomes You

Label:	**Written by:**	**Length:**
Brunswick	Van Heusen / Burke	3 mins 9 secs

Bing Crosby was the first real multimedia star and a leader in record sales, radio ratings, and motion picture grosses from 1931 to 1954. His early career coincided with recording innovations that allowed him to develop an intimate singing style that influenced many male singers who followed him including Perry Como, Frank Sinatra, Dick Haymes, and Dean Martin. For his achievements Crosby has been recognised with three stars on the Hollywood Walk of Fame; for motion pictures, radio, and audio recording.

Bert Ambrose & His Orchestra
The Sailor With The Navy Blue Eyes

Label:	**Written by:**	**Length:**
Decca	Taylor / Mizzy / Hoffman	2 mins 57 secs

Benjamin Baruch Ambrose (b. 11th September 1896 - d. 11th June 1971) was a bandleader and violinist who became the leader of the highly acclaimed British dance band Bert Ambrose & His Orchestra in the 1930s. Known professionally as Ambrose or Bert Ambrose, his major discovery in the years leading up to the war was the singer Vera Lynn, who sang with his band from 1937 to 1940.

Glenn Miller
Moonlight Cocktail

Label:	Written by:	Length:
Bluebird	Roberts / Gannon	3 mins 14 secs

Alton Glenn Miller (b. 1st March 1904 - MIA 15th December 1944) was a big-band musician, arranger, composer and bandleader. He was the best-selling recording artist from 1939 to 1943, leading one of the most popular and commercially successful dance orchestras of the swing era.

The Andrews Sisters
Pennsylvania Polka

Label:	Written by:	Length:
Decca	Lee / Manners	2 mins 49 secs

The Andrews Sisters were a close harmony singing group from the eras of swing and boogie-woogie. The group consisted of three sisters: LaVerne Sophia (b. 6th July 1911 - d. 8th May 1967), Maxene Angelyn (b. 3rd January 1916 - d. 21st October 1995) and Patricia Marie (b. 16th February 1918 - d. 30th January 2013). Throughout their long career the sisters sold over 75 million records.

1942: TOP FILMS

1. **Mrs. Miniver** - *Metro-Goldwyn-Mayer*
2. **Yankee Doodle Dandy** - *Warner Bros.*
3. **Random Harvest** - *Metro-Goldwyn-Mayer*
4. **Reap the Wild Wind** - *Paramount Pictures*
5. **Holiday Inn** - *Paramount Pictures*

OSCARS

Best Picture: Mrs. Miniver
Most Nominations: Mrs. Miniver (12)
Most Wins: Mrs. Miniver (6)

Oscar winners (from left): Heflin, Garson, Cagney and Wright.

Best Director: William Wyler - *Mrs. Miniver*

Best Actor: James Cagney - *Yankee Doodle Dandy*
Best Actress: Greer Garson - *Mrs. Miniver*
Best Supporting Actor: Van Heflin - *Johnny Eager*
Best Supporting Actress: Teresa Wright - *Mrs. Miniver*

The 15th Academy Awards, honouring the best in film for 1942, were presented on the 4th March 1943 at The Ambassador Hotel in Los Angeles, California.

MRS. MINIVER

Greer GARSON
Walter PIDGEON

VOTED THE GREATEST MOVIE EVER MADE!

DUNKIRK
RAF

Directed by
WILLIAM WYLER
Produced by
SIDNEY FRANKLIN

MRS. MINIVER

with TERESA WRIGHT · DAME MAY WHITTY
REGINALD OWEN · HENRY TRAVERS
RICHARD NEY · HENRY WILCOXON

SCREEN PLAY BY ARTHUR WIMPERIS, GEORGE FROESCHEL, JAMES HILTON AND CLAUDINE WEST

IN A WILLIAM WYLER PRODUCTION BASED ON JAN STRUTHER'S NOVEL

Directed by: William Wyler - Runtime: 2h 14m

The Minivers, an English middle-class family, experience life in the first months of World War II.

Starring

Greer Garson
b. 29th September 1904
d. 6th April 1966
Character:
Mrs. Miniver

Walter Pidgeon
b. 23rd September 1897
d. 25th September 1984
Character:
Clem Miniver

Teresa Wright
b. 27th October 1918
d. 6th March 2005
Character:
Carol Beldon

Trivia

Goof	In the radio broadcast by Lord Haw Haw he mentions the fall of France. A day or so later the boats are called out to help in the evacuation of Dunkirk (Operation Dynamo). France did not fall until two weeks after Dunkirk.
Interesting Facts	After first-choice Norma Shearer rejected the title role of Mrs. Miniver because she refused to play a mother, Greer Garson was cast. Although Garson didn't want the part either she was contractually bound to take it and won her only Oscar for her performance. *NB: Garson was nominated a total of 7 times for the Academy Award for Best Actress throughout her career.*
	Winston Churchill once said that this film had done more for the war effort than a flotilla of destroyers.
	After completing the film, William Wyler joined the U.S. Army and was overseas on the night he won his first Oscar. He later revealed that his subsequent war experiences made him realise that the film actually portrayed war in too soft a light. *NB: Wyler went on to win two more Academy Awards for Best Director; The Best Years of Our Lives (1946), Ben-Hur (1959).*
	Shortly after shooting was completed, Greer Garson married Richard Ney, who plays her son, Vin, in the film.
	Mrs. Miniver is first of only two Academy Award Best Picture winners to receive nominations in all four acting categories. The other is From Here to Eternity (1953).
Quote	**Carol Beldon**: I know how comfortable it is to curl up with a nice, fat book full of big words and think you're going to solve all the problems in the universe. But you're not, you know. A bit of action is required every now and then.

Directed by: Michael Curtiz - Runtime: 2h 6m

The life of the renowned musical composer, playwright, actor, dancer and singer, George M. Cohan.

Starring

James Cagney
b. 17th July 1899
d. 30th March 1986
Character:
George M. Cohan

Joan Leslie
b. 26th January 1925
d. 12th October 2015
Character:
Mary Cohan

Walter Huston
b. 5th April 1883
d. 7th April 1950
Character:
Jerry Cohan

Trivia

Goof

In the "You're A Grand Old Flag" number, which supposedly takes place in the 1906 production of George Washington Jr., we see a group of Boy Scouts march onto the stage. The Scout Movement was founded in 1907 by Robert Baden-Powell in England and wasn't founded in the United States until 1910.

Interesting Facts

Despite failing health, the real George M. Cohan acted briefly as a consultant on the film. He lived long enough to see the finished result and approved wholeheartedly of James Cagney's depiction of himself.

Joan Leslie portrays Mary Cohan, aging from 18 to 57 throughout proceedings. Leslie turned 17 during the production of the film. The fact that she was still attending school during filming caused numerous delays.

Future director Don Siegel was responsible for putting together the numerous montages that appear throughout the film.

James Cagney became the first actor to win the Best Actor Academy Award for a musical performance.

According to his biography the rather stiff-legged dancing style used by James Cagney in this film is not his own. He copied George M. Cohan's style to make the film more accurate.

Quotes

[first lines]
Critic #1: I call it a hit. What'll your review say?
Critic #2: I like it too, so I guess I'll pan it. it.

George M. Cohan: My mother thanks you, my father thanks you, my sister thanks you, and I thank you.

Directed by: Mervyn LeRoy - Runtime: 2h 6m

An amnesiac World War I veteran falls in love with a music hall star, only to suffer an accident which restores his original memories but erases his post-war life.

Starring

Ronald Colman
b. 9th February 1891
d. 19th May 1958
Character:
Charles Rainier /
"John Smith" (Smithy)

Greer Garson
b. 29th September 1904
d. 6th April 1966
Character:
"Paula Ridgeway" /
Margaret Hanson

Philip Dorn
b. 30th September 1901
d. 9th May 1975
Character:
Dr. Jonathan Benet

Trivia

Goof | In the last scene where Smithy goes back to the cottage, the flowering tree on the path has not changed or grown at all in the 15 years since he was last there.

Interesting Facts | The person Greer Garson spent the most time with on set was cameraman Joseph Ruttenberg who was her favourite photographer. She appreciated his using a woman's stocking over the lens to soften and glamourise her features. In addition, he quickly realised that she looked best shot from the right and made sure the sets were constructed so he could favour that side.

Like most Hollywood films of the era, it was shot entirely on a studio backlot, where designers and technicians created their own versions of the streets of Liverpool, London's Waterloo Station and the cottage where Paula and Smithy found happiness.

When the writers had trouble coming up with a scene to show Paula on stage, Greer Garson suggested singing the Harry Lauder standard "She M' Daisy" in a short kilt. Sidney Franklin and Louis B. Mayer hesitated, concerned that the show of leg would hurt her image as the perfect lady. They even tried kilts in three different lengths, finally choosing a medium-length one that wouldn't show too much leg.

Ronald Colman had first-hand experience of shell shock - he had fought in the British army at the Battle of Ypres in World War I, during which he was also gassed.

Quote | **Smithy**: I don't even know who I am.
Paula: Well, I know who you are. You're someone awfully nice.

REAP THE WILD WIND

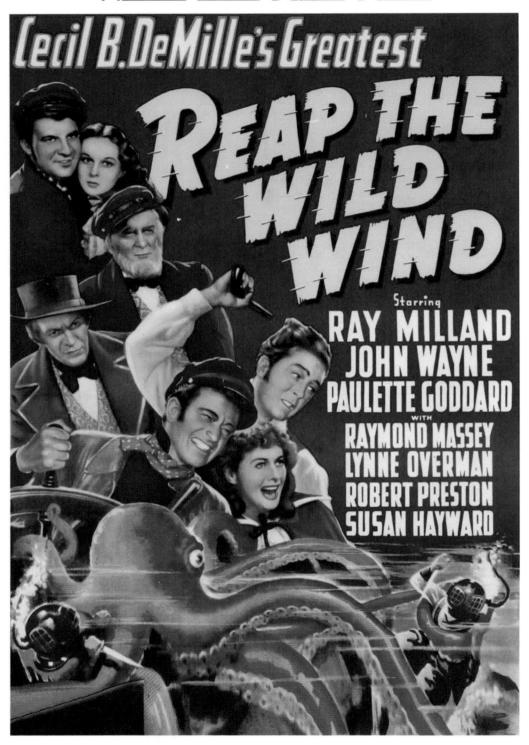

Directed by: Cecil B. DeMille - Runtime: 2h 3m

Florida ship salvager Loxi Claiborne falls for Jack Stuart, the captain of a ship wrecked on the Key West shore. However, their romance is complicated by the arrival of another suitor, and eventually leads to tragedy.

Starring

Ray Milland

b. 3rd January 1907
d. 10th March 1986
Character:
Stephen Tolliver

John Wayne

b. 26th May 1907
d. 11th June 1979
Character:
Jack Stuart

Paulette Goddard

b. 3rd June 1910
d. 23rd April 1990
Character:
Loxi Claiborne

Trivia

Goofs | The first time Loxi talks to Jack, her hat ribbon repeatedly changes position around her neck between shots. The second time Loxi talks to Jack, she points at him with the index finger of her left hand. In the next shot it is her right hand.

Interesting Facts | John Wayne did not like Cecil B. DeMille. He felt the director had passed him over for the role of Wild Bill Hickok in The Plainsman (1936), which Wayne had felt certain would have made him a star.

Cecil B. DeMille had wanted Errol Flynn to play Captain Jack Stuart, but Jack L. Warner refused to loan him out.

The shots of the giant squid wrapping its tentacles around the actors was done by wrapping the actors in the tentacles, then unwrapping them and showing the film in reverse. *NB: The rubber squid was donated by the studio to the war effort in 1942 because the Japanese had conquered Malaya and Indochina, the source of most of the world's rubber.*

Although John Wayne was pleased to have been cast in such an important film, he was unhappy with his part and once complained he was only there to make Ray Milland look like a "real man".

During the filming of a fight scene with John Wayne, an accident cost actor Victor Kilian (Widgeon) the use of one eye.

For the 1954 theatrical re-release, John Wayne was given top billing in the posters because of his increased star status, and Susan Hayward, who had become a major star instead of a supporting player, was misleadingly billed second. Formerly top-billed Ray Milland got third billing in the new posters, whilst leading lady Paulette Goddard was demoted to fourth billing.

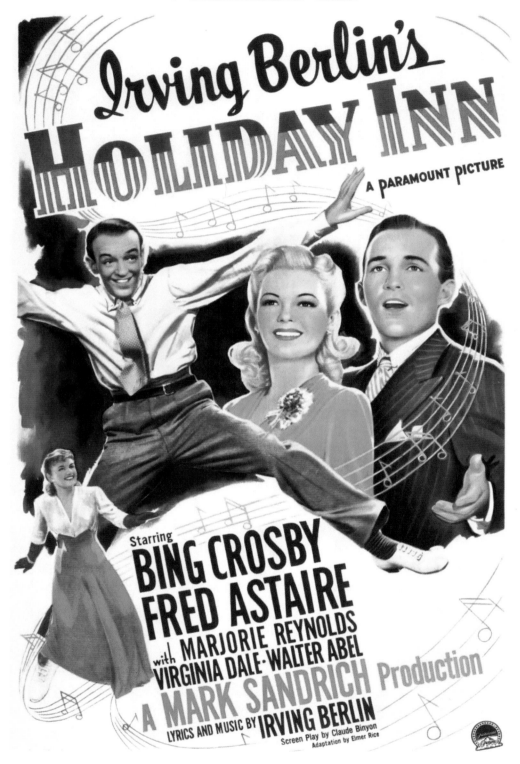

Directed by: Mark Sandrich - Runtime: 1h 40m

At an inn which is open only on holidays, a crooner and a dancer vie for the affections of a beautiful up-and-coming performer.

Starring

Bing Crosby
b. 3rd May 1903
d. 14th October 1977
Character:
Jim Hardy

Fred Astaire
b. 10th May 1899
d. 22nd June 1987
Character:
Ted Hanover

Marjorie Reynolds
b. 12th August 1917
d. 1st February 1997
Character:
Linda Mason

Trivia

Goof	When Jim first plays "White Christmas" with Linda at the inn, he sits down to play a piano. However, there is no piano present on the audio track.
Interesting Facts	Director Mark Sandrich originally wanted Ginger Rogers and Rita Hayworth as the female leads. However, executives at Paramount vetoed this idea, since Bing Crosby and Fred Astaire, two of the studio's highest-paid stars, were already co-starring in the film.
	For the "drunk" dance, Fred Astaire had two drinks of bourbon before the first take and one before each succeeding take. The seventh and last take was eventually used in the film.
	Both of the leading ladies have their hair dyed opposite to their natural hair colour: Marjorie Reynolds is a brunette playing the blonde Linda Mason; Virginia Dale is a blonde playing brunette Lila Dixon.
	When Irving Berlin won an Oscar for his song "White Christmas" he became the first ever artist to present himself with an Academy Award.
	The Connecticut Inn set for this film was reused by Paramount 12 years later as a Vermont Inn for the musical White Christmas (1954), also starring Bing Crosby and again with songs composed by Irving Berlin.
	The "Holiday Inn" motel chain (established in 1952) was named after this film.
Quote	**Linda Mason**: What would you like? **Danny Reed**: Orchids, the finest you've got. **Linda Mason**: Corsage? **Danny Reed**: No, no. A dozen, loose, looking like they don't care!

SPORTING WINNERS

Football

Between 1939 and 1946 normal competitive football was suspended in England and Scotland. Many footballers had signed up to fight in the war leaving teams depleted.

England: The 1941-1942 season was the third season of special wartime football in England. The Football League and FA Cup had been suspended and replaced with regional competitions. League competition was split into two, North and South, however London clubs organised their own competitions. Teams played as many fixtures as was feasible and winners were decided on point average rather than total. Appearances in these tournaments did not count in players' official records.

Competition	Winner
League North (1st Championship)	Blackpool
League North (2nd Championship)	Manchester United
League South	Leicester City
London League	Arsenal
Football League War Cup	Wolverhampton Wanderers
London War Cup	Brentford

Scotland: The 1941-1942 season was the third season of special wartime football in Scotland. The Scottish Football League and Scottish Cup were suspended and, in their place, regional league competitions were set up. Appearances in these tournaments did not count in players' official records.

Competition	Winner
Southern League	Rangers
North-Eastern League (Autumn)	Rangers
North-Eastern League (Spring)	Aberdeen
Glasgow Cup	Rangers
East of Scotland Shield	Hearts
Renfrewshire Cup	Morton
Southern League Cup	Rangers
Summer Cup	Rangers
North-Eastern League Cup (Autumn)	Aberdeen
North-Eastern League Cup (Spring)	Dundee United

International Matches

Five unofficial international football matches were played in 1942 between England, Scotland and Wales. During this period no caps were awarded.

17th Jan	England	3-0	Scotland
18th Apr	Scotland	5-4	England
9th May	Wales	1-0	England
10th Oct	England	0-0	Scotland
24th Oct	England	1-2	Wales

Rugby - Home Nations

The 1942 Home Nations Championship series was not contested due to the war. International rugby was put on hold and would not resume again until 1947, when the Home Nations would become the Five Nations with the addition of France to the line-up.

Horse Racing

Grand National: Although the Grand National was run as normal in 1940 and most other major horse races around the world were able to be held throughout the war, the commandeering of Aintree for defence use in 1941 meant the Grand National could not be held between 1941 and 1945.

The Derby Stakes is Britain's richest horse race and the most prestigious of the country's five Classics. First run in 1780 this Group 1 flat horse race is open to three year old thoroughbred colts and fillies. Although the race usually takes place at Epsom Downs in Surrey, during both World Wars the venue was changed and the Derby was run at Newmarket - these races are known as the "New Derby". *Note: Epsom Downs racecourse was used for an anti-aircraft battery throughout World War II.*

Watling Street Derby 1942
Churchill 'A' Series

Winner	Jockey	Trainer	Owner	Prize Money
Watling Street	Harry Wragg	Walter Earl	17th Earl of Derby	£3,844

Golf - Open Championship

The Open Championship was cancelled in 1942 due to the war and the tournament was not contested again until 1946.

Tennis - Wimbledon

The 1942 Wimbledon Championships was another sporting event cancelled due to World War II. Hosted since 1877 by the All England Lawn Tennis and Croquet Club in Wimbledon, London, the competition did not resume again until 1946.

County Cricket

All first-class cricket was cancelled during the Second World War. No first-class matches were played in England after Friday, 1st September 1939 (cricket would resume again on Saturday, 19th May 1945).

World Snooker Championship

The World Snooker Championship was cancelled because of the war and would not be held again until 1946.

THE COST OF LIUING

KEEPS WAR WORKERS "FIGHTING FIT"

On a Man's Job—and equal to it

Of course she's tired at the end of the day, but not "played out." Her power of endurance is amazing and, as she would tell you, this is because she so regularly includes Weetabix in her meals. Every crumb of Weetabix is sheer nourishment, because Weetabix is the *whole* of the wheat with *all* its valuable mineral salts and vitamins intact.

Ready to eat; delicious alone or with anything in the larder; and especially a boon to those who have to snatch a meal when and where they can.

Weetabix
More than a breakfast food

Weetabix Ltd., Burton Latimer, Northants.
WX4

| SMALL SIZE 2 POINTS | 7½D |
| LARGE SIZE 4 POINTS | 1/1D |

Comparison Chart

	1942	1942 (+ Inflation)	2021	% Change
3 Bedroom House	£1,000	£50,816	£235,243	+362.9%
Weekly Income	£3.1s.2d	£155.41	£621	+299.6%
Pint Of Beer	9d	£1.91	£3.94	+106.3%
Cheese (lb)	1s.7d	£4.02	£3.04	-24.4%
Bacon (lb)	1s.10d	£4.66	£3.20	-31.3%
The Beano	2d	42p	£2.75	+554.8%

Shopping

Dried Eggs (tin, 12 eggs)	1s.9d
Kia-Ora Orange Cordial	2s.6d
Rowntree's Cocoa (½lb)	9½d
Bournville Cocoa (¼lb)	5d
Peppermint Cream	2½d
Walters' Palm Toffee (¼lb)	5d
Toffee Cream	3d
Syminton's Soup (packet)	2d
Ryvita Bread (packet)	10d
Evan Williams Shampoo (packet)	5d
Palmolive Soap (tablet)	3½d
Lux Toilet Soap (tablet)	3½d
Radox	1s.10½d
Spa Toothbrush	1s.9½d
S. R. Toothpaste (large tube)	1s.3d
Colgate Toothpaste (large tube)	1s.1d
Tangee Lipstick Refill	1s.10d
Rennies (25)	7d
Dinneford's Pure Fluid Magnesia	1s.5d
Dr. Cassell's Nerve Tablets	1s.4d
Do-Do Asthma Tablets (7 doses)	1s
Cephos Colds & Flu Remedy	1s.3d
Vapex Cold Cure	2s.3d
Tampax Sanitary Protection	7d
Grasshopper Ointment	7d
Lux Washing Powder (6oz packet)	4d
Thawpit Fabric Stain Remover	1s

Clothes

Women's Clothing

Smartwear Jigger Coat	7½gns
J. A. Davis & Co Woollen Coat	£5.5s
Artificial Silk Gloves	15s.11d
Harvey Nichols Checked Winter Suit	£15.10s.9d
C&A Junior Miss Dress	19s.11d
Barkers Utility Stockings	2s
Lilley & Skinner Utility Court Shoe	£1.6s.8d
Suede Wedge Heel Indoor Shoes	£2.17s.6d

Men's Clothing

Austin Reed Great Coat	10gns
Man's Finest Cloth Suit	5gns
Wilson Brothers Busmen's Suit	£1.12s.6d
Balaklava Heavy-weight Work Trousers	11s.6d
Army Boots	10s.6d

COLUMBIA RECORDS

The Biggest Names in Dance Music

CARROLL GIBBONS
and The Savoy Hotel Orpheans

Rustic Rhapsodie
Two in Love } FB 2777

No More ; By Candlelight - FB 2778

Tropical Man ; The man
with the Lollypop Song } FB 2763

Time was ; Elmer's Tune - FB 2764

... at the Piano

Carroll Calls the Tunes,
No. 18 } FB 2768

VICTOR SILVESTER
and his Ballroom Orchestra

Baby Mine ; Two in Love - FB 2775

Elmer's Tune
Anniversary Waltz } FB 2776

Do you Care ?
That lovely Week-end } FB 2755

Green Eyes ; Babette - - FB 2756

Victor Silvester's Strings for Dancing

Die Fledermaus, Waltz
Unrequited Love, Waltz } FB 2773

JOHNNY CLAES
and his Clae-Pigeons

The Whistler's Mother-
in-Law ; Watch the
Birdie } FB 2774

Nobody knows de
trouble I've Seen
Chattanooga Choo-Choo } FB 2765

FELIX MENDELSSOHN
and his Hawaiian Serenaders

Love Everlasting
La Cucaracha } FB 2772

Solitude ; Mood Indigo FB 2753

FB 10-in. 2/6 (+ 6½d. Tax)
DB 10-in. 3/3 (+ 8½d. Tax)

TURNER LAYTON

Baby Mine
By Candlelight } FB 2771

The world will sing again
He wants to be a Pilot } FB 2750

MONTE REY

So Suddenly ; Green Eyes - FB 2769

DELYA

Scottish Song Memories - FB 2766

BING CROSBY

Waltzing in a Dream
We'll make Hay while
the Sun Shines } DB 2074

BILLIE CAMPBELL

By Candlelight
Greetings from You } FB 2779

Jimmy Leach and the
NEW "ORGANOLIANS"

When I see an Elephant
Fly ; Rustic Rhapsodie } FB 2770

FODEN'S MOTOR WORKS BAND
Conducted by Fred Mortimer

Song of the Fatherland
Soviet Airmen's Song } FB 2767

GRENADIER GUARDS BAND
Cond. Lt.-Col. George Miller

Star Spangled
Banner
Invincible Eagle,
March } DB 2072

COLUMBIA GRAPHOPHONE CO.   LIMITED, HAYES, MIDDLESEX

Other Prices

Suit Dry Cleaning & Tailor Pressing	1s.9d
Osbaldiston's Ladies Shopping Bag	3s.6d
Gents Hide Leather Dressing Case	25s
Ladies Brush Set	10s.6d
Lewis's Ready Mixed Paint (5lb tin)	2s
Oak Finish Table Lamp	1gn
Penn's Instant Firelighter	2s.4d
Furmoto Non-Slip Floor Cream	2s
Booth's Dry Gin (half bottle)	11s.9d
Seagers Cocktails	12s.6d
Wincarnis Tonic Wine (pint)	4s.9d
Burlington Cigars (half corona)	1s
Player's Digger Flake Tobacco (1oz)	1s.3½d
Capstan Navy Cut Cigarettes (20)	1s.5½d
Craven 'A' Cigarettes (10)	9d
Midget Patience Playing Cards	4s.6d
Woman's Weekly Magazine	3d

Money Conversion Table

Pounds / Shillings / Pence 'Old Money'		Decimal Value	Value 2021 (Rounded)
Farthing	¼d	0.1p	5p
Half Penny	½d	0.21p	11p
Penny	1d	0.42p	21p
Threepence	3d	1.25p	64p
Sixpence	6d	2.5p	£1.27
Shilling	1s	5p	£2.54
Florin	2s	10p	£5.08
Half Crown	2s.6d	12.5p	£6.35
Crown	5s	25p	£12.70
Ten Shillings	10s	50p	£25.41
Pound	20s	£1	£50.82
Guinea	21s	£1.05	£53.36
Five Pounds	£5	£5	£254.08
Ten Pounds	£10	£10	£508.16

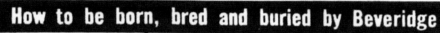

How to be born, bred and buried by Beveridge

ON MARRIAGE
—there's a lump sum of up to **£10**

ON BECOMING A MOTHER
there's a lump sum of **£4** —and for three months there's **36/-** a week for those who had paid jobs.

THE CHILDREN ARE CARED FOR—
8s. a week
is allowed you whether you are in work or not—for every child under 16, except the first.

IN CASE OF ILLNESS
there's medical, dental, and hospital treatment to be had by all.

ON GETTING BURIED
there's a funeral grant of

£20 for adults
£6 if under 3 **£10** if under 10 **£15** if under 20

THERE'S PROVISION FOR WIDOWS—
Widows and separated wives are to get enough to live on and bring up their children. Young childless widows will be given training for employment.

And there's a happy old age for Darby and Joan

On retirement (ages 65 for men, 60 for women)

there's a sum rising to 24s. for a single person | and a sum rising to 40s. for man and wife

If you do not retire at 65 you will increase your pension by 2s. a week for each year you go on working.

Printed in Great Britain
by Amazon